JAN 1 5

A French Cookbook for Kids

Rosemary Hankin

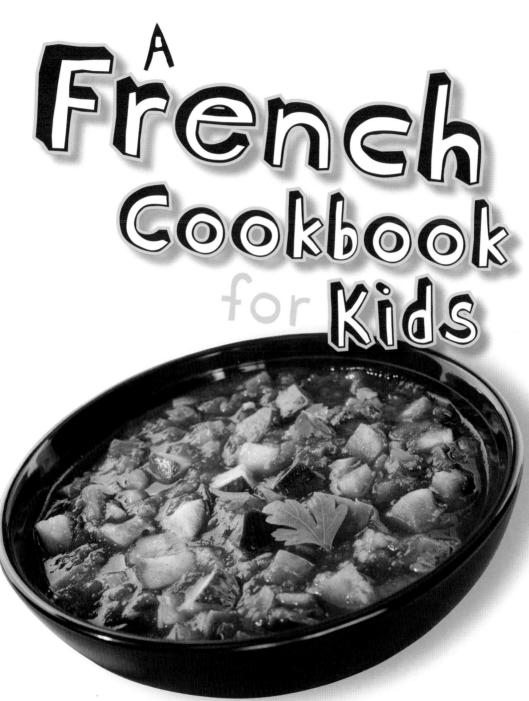

PowerKiDS press

New York

Published in 2014 by The Rosen Publishing Group, Inc.
29 East 21st Street, New York, NY 10010

Produced for Rosen by Calcium Creative Ltd
Editor for Calcium Creative Ltd: Sarah Eason
US Editor: Sara Howell
Designer: Paul Myerscough

Photo credits: Cover: Shutterstock: Apollofoto. Inside: Dreamstime: Galina Barskaya 6l, Enrico Carlone 21t, Charles Knox Photo 25b, Cynoclub 21b, Flynt 25t, Andreas Karelias 17t, Pipa100 7l, Silencefoto 17b, Yurchyk 7r; Shutterstock: AB Images 14, Africa Studio 26, S Borisov 5bl, CandyBox Images 6r, Brian Dicks 13t, Nikolay Dimitrov 5tl, Elen Studio 5tr, Food Pictures 22, Netfalls / Remy Musser 9b, Nayashkova Olga 10, Jose Ignacio Soto 9t, Travellight 18, Yeko Photo Studio 5c; Tudor Photography: 11, 15, 19, 23, 27.

Library of Congress Cataloging-in-Publication Data

Hankin, Rosemary.
 A French cookbook for kids / by Rosemary Hankin.
    pages cm. — (Cooking around the world)
 Includes index.
 ISBN 978-1-4777-1337-2 (library binding) — ISBN 978-1-4777-1522-2 (pbk.) — ISBN 978-1-4777-1523-9 (6-pack)
 1. Cooking, French—Juvenile literature. I. Title.
 TX719.H2639 2014
 641.5944—dc23
                                  2013003792

Manufactured in the United States of America

CPSIA Compliance Information: Batch #S13PK8: For Further Information contact Rosen Publishing, New York, New York at 1-800-237-9932

Contents

Fabulous France

What do you think of when you hear the name "France?" Perhaps you think about Paris, the capital city, and its buildings such as the Eiffel Tower or Notre Dame Cathedral.

Most people think of food when you say France because the country is famous for its delicious cooking. Well-known French dishes include onion soup, which is made with slow-cooked onion. *Tarte tatin* is a famous French apple pie. Also on the menu are freshly made, crusty baguettes, or French bread, and flaky, buttery **croissants**.

The French are famous for their wonderful cheeses such as creamy Brie and Camembert, and their goat-milk cheese called Chèvre. In France, cheese is served after the main course but before dessert. The country also makes lots of different wines to go with all the tasty food. The best sparkling wine in the world, champagne, is made in France.

Different types of cheese are made in different parts of France.

France is famous for its southern coastline, where the Cannes Film **Festival** is held.

The Eiffel Tower is one of the most famous buildings in Paris.

5

Get Set to Cook

Cooking is fun! There is nothing better than making food and then sharing it with your family and friends.

Every recipe page in this book starts with a "You Will Need" list. This is a set of **ingredients**. Be sure to collect everything on the list before you start cooking.

Look out for the "Top Tips" boxes. These have great tips to help you cook.

"Be Safe!" boxes warn you when you need to be extra careful.

Use one cutting board for meat and fish and a different cutting board for vegetables and fruit.

Always ask a grown-up if you can do some cooking.

Watch out for sharp knives! Ask a grown-up to help you with chopping and slicing.

Be sure to wash your hands before you start cooking.

Always wash any fruit and vegetables before using them.

Always ask a grown-up for help when cooking on the stove or using the oven.

Wear an apron to keep your clothes clean as you cook.

Famous Paris

The capital of France is the beautiful city of Paris, which is in the north of the country. There are many places to visit in Paris, including the Champs-Élysées and Montmartre. The Seine River runs through Paris and many visitors to the city see its **sites** by taking a boat trip down the river.

Eating in the City

There are many places to eat in Paris. It is said that there are over 9,000 restaurants in the city! There are also lots of cafés, with tables and chairs on the sidewalks.

Shopping for Food

Different shops in France sell different types of food. Prepared meats and **pâtés** can be found in the *charcuterie*. The *fromagerie* sells cheese. The *boulangerie* sells freshly baked bread every day. The *patisserie* is where you can buy delicious French desserts and pastries. There are many open-air and covered markets in Paris. These sell fruit and vegetables, fish and meat, cheeses, and all sorts of bread.

Amazing **gargoyles** decorate Notre Dame Cathedral in Paris.

Lots of different types of bread can be bought in the boulangerie.

Croque Madame

YOU WILL NEED:

2 tbsp Dijon mustard
8 slices white bread
4 ounces (113 g) ham,
   thinly sliced
2½ cups Gruyère cheese, grated
4 tbsp butter, softened
4 eggs
2 tbsp corn oil
fresh lettuce, to **garnish**
black pepper, to taste

Little cafés throughout France sell delicious *croque madames*. This tasty snack is a sandwich made with ham and cheese and a fried egg on top. This recipe makes four mouth-watering sandwiches. Enjoy!

BE SAFE!
• Ask a grown-up to help you when using the broiler.
• Be careful when using the pan.

STEP 1

Preheat the broiler to the lowest setting. Spread the mustard onto four slices of bread. Place the ham on top. Add the cheese and cover it with the remaining slices of bread. Spread the butter on the outside of the sandwiches.

STEP 2

Place the sandwiches on an ungreased baking sheet and broil for 5 minutes. Turn the sandwiches over and continue cooking the bread for another 5 minutes, until it is crispy and golden brown.

STEP 3

Meanwhile, heat the oil in a pan over a medium heat to fry the eggs while the sandwiches broil. Fry one egg at a time.

STEP 4

Remove the sandwiches from the baking sheet and place on plates, then top with the eggs. Cool for 10 minutes before serving, then add black pepper to taste and garnish with fresh lettuce.

TOP TIP Try your sandwich with a little béchamel sauce spooned over it, too.

11

Into Lorraine

Lorraine is a region in northeast France. The main city, Metz, is one of the oldest in France and the remains of the **medieval** city can still be seen today. Nancy is one of Lorraine's most important cities and has an enormous city square called Place Stanislas. As well as having many famous cities, Lorraine is also famous because Joan of Arc was born here.

Famous Food

Lorraine's most famous dish is **quiche** Lorraine, which is now baked and enjoyed all over the world. Its three basic ingredients are bacon, cream, and eggs. Lorraine hotpot is a slow-cooked stew of bacon, beans, and smoked sausage. Herbs and vegetables, such as potatoes, leeks, **rutabaga**, carrots, and cabbage are also added to the hotpot.

Sweet Treats

Lorraine is famous for its small, yellow mirabelle plums. They are eaten fresh or made into jellies and used in mirabelle tarts. Almond cookies, or macaroons, are made in Nancy and madeleine cakes are made in Liverdun. Every December, at the Feast of St. Nicolas, gingerbread is given as a special treat to children who have been good!

Nancy has lots of wonderful medieval buildings to visit.

Mirabelle plums are yellow in color and sometimes dotted with red. They are used in many different dishes in Lorraine.

Quiche Lorraine

YOU WILL NEED:

For the Pastry

1½ cups all-purpose flour
1 stick (½ cup) butter, diced
1 egg yolk
dry beans

For the Filling

7 ounces (198 g) bacon pieces, cooked
2 ounces (56 g) Gruyère, three-quarters
    diced, the remaining grated
1 cup sour cream
1 cup heavy cream
2 eggs, beaten
pinch of nutmeg,
    grated

Quiche Lorraine is named for the Lorraine region of northeast France that it comes from. This dish is now popular all across France and around the world. Serve it with a salad and homemade **vinaigrette** dressing.

BE SAFE!
- Ask a grown-up to help you to make the pastry.
- Always be very careful when using the oven.

14

STEP 1

Mix the flour, butter, and egg yolk together. Then roll out onto a floured surface and line a 9 inch (22 cm) loose-based, fluted pie pan with the dough. Trim the edges. Prick the base with a fork, then chill for 10 minutes. In the oven, heat a baking sheet to 400°F (200°C).

STEP 2

Line the pie crust with foil, fill with the dry beans, and bake on the hot baking sheet for 15 minutes. Remove the foil and beans and bake for 4–5 minutes more. Set aside.

TOP TIP You can also use ready-made pastry dough. Roll out according to the packet instructions.

STEP 3

Scatter the diced cheese and bacon over the pie crust.

STEP 4

Beat together the sour cream, heavy cream, nutmeg, and eggs. Pour into the pie crust. Scatter the grated cheese over.

STEP 5

Place the quiche on the hot baking sheet. Lower the oven to 375°F (190°C). Bake for 25 minutes, until golden. Remove from the oven and let it sit for 5 minutes before serving.

Pretty Provence

With the Alps to the north and the Mediterranean to the south, Provence is a lovely part of France. It is so pretty that many famous artists, including Vincent Van Gogh and Paul Cézanne, painted here. Provence is especially famous for its fields of flowers.

Cooking with Herbs

Dishes cooked in Provence are made with olive oil, onions, garlic, tomatoes, and herbs. *Herbes de Provence* is a special mix of herbs including thyme, rosemary, marjoram, sage, basil, mint, and another type of mint called savory.

Fishy Food

Lots of people in Provence like to eat fish, especially on the coast. A famous fish dish is bouillabaisse. It is a soup of mixed fish flavored with fennel, garlic, bitter orange, and a pinch of saffron. It is served with garlic mayonnaise.

Fun Festivals

The people of Provence love to celebrate food! In one part of Provence they even have a competition to see which village can make the best-tasting soup. A chestnut festival is also held in Var every October.

Provence flower fields are full of beautiful sunflowers and lavender.

People in Provence love to eat delicious bouillabaisse with crusty fresh bread.

Ratatouille

YOU WILL NEED:

4 tbsp olive oil

1 pound (453 g) eggplant,
  cut into chunks

1 pound (453 g) zucchini,
  cut into chunks

½ pound (226 g) onion,
  peeled and chopped

2 garlic cloves, minced

salt and ground black pepper,
  to taste

1 pound (453 g) tomatoes,
  firm and ripe

3 tbsp fresh parsley,
  chopped

This famous French dish has many different recipes. Some are very simple, like this one. Others contain added ingredients, such as bell peppers. Fresh herbs, such as basil, also add lots of flavor.

BE SAFE!
- Ask a grown-up to help you chop the vegetables.
- The tomatoes should be peeled by a grown-up.

18

STep 1

Heat 2 tbsp olive oil in a skillet. **Sauté** the eggplant and zucchini, stirring, for 2 minutes. Set aside.

STep 2

Heat the remaining oil and use it to cook the onions over a medium heat for 10 minutes. Stir in the garlic and add salt and ground black pepper.

TOP TIP This dish may be served hot or cold, with plenty of fresh crusty bread.

STep 3

To peel the tomatoes, plunge them into boiling water for 30 seconds. Remove from the water and take the skin off using a small, sharp knife. Cut into chunks and add to the onions. Cover and cook over a low heat for 5 minutes. Uncover, increase the heat, and boil for 10 minutes more.

STep 4

Combine all the vegetables in a pot. Sprinkle with the parsley. Cover and simmer over a low heat for around 10 minutes. Uncover and increase the heat then cook for around 15 minutes, stirring occasionally.

Wild Auvergne

In the center of France is the Massif Central. This is a huge, wild area where **volcanoes** once erupted. The Massif Central has high rocky places and deep **gorges**. Auvergne is found in this part of France.

Country Food

Pigs are farmed in Auvergne and many types of sausages eaten in the area are made from pork. Fresh pork is often cooked with potatoes and vegetables to make a stew.

Cooking for Energy

In the past, life in Auvergne was tough. Food became very important here because people needed a lot of energy to survive in the wild landscape. Now, people fill up on good food to fuel themselves for the many fun sports that take place in Auvergne.

Sharp and Nutty

The people of Auvergne make lots of cheeses. One famous cheese from the area is *Fourme d'Ambert*. It has a nutty, fruity taste, and it is eaten with apples or pears.

There are lots of amazing sports in Auvergne. Skiing, rafting, and hang gliding are all popular.

Sharp-tasting, blue cheeses, such as *Bleu d'Auvergne*, are very popular in Auvergne.

Truffade

YOU WILL NEED:

2¼ pounds (1.02 kg) medium
   size potatoes
1 tbsp lard
2 onions, peeled and sliced
1 garlic clove, minced
4 ounces (113 g) bacon,
   chopped
14 ounces (396 g) Tomme
   cheese, thinly sliced
salt and ground black pepper,
   to taste
fresh parsley, chopped,
   to garnish

Truffade is easy to make. It uses sliced, shredded, or mashed potatoes sprinkled with cheese. It is then fried with bacon and garlic. It can be eaten on its own but is also often served with meat.

BE SAFE!
• Be careful when you are peeling and slicing the potatoes.
• Ask a grown-up to help you when cooking on the stove.

STEP 1

Peel the potatoes and cut them into thick slices. Cook them in salted, boiling water until they are just firm. Remove them from the pan and set aside.

STEP 2

Heat the lard in a skillet. Sauté the sliced onions, stirring occasionally, for 5 minutes or until softened. Stir in the minced garlic and sauté for a few minutes longer, stirring.

STEP 3

Add the chopped bacon. Stir to combine and cook thoroughly. Then add the potato slices. Cook until they are browned, turning occasionally.

STEP 4

Cover the potato mixture with the slices of Tomme. When the cheese has melted, add salt and ground black pepper to taste. The base of the truffade should be beginning to crisp. Sprinkle with the chopped fresh parsley before serving.

TOP TIP Use Cheddar, Gruyère, or Monterey Jack cheese if you cannot find Tomme in a grocery store.

Beautiful Brittany

Brittany is the most western part of France, and it has a very long, pretty coastline. The shores have hundreds of bays and **inlets** and people have fished there for hundreds, probably thousands, of years.

Ancient Abbey

Mont-Saint-Michel is a medieval **abbey** on a rocky island off the coast of southern Brittany. It took a long time to create the abbey, which was built between the eleventh and sixteenth centuries. You reach this amazing place only by walking across the beach to it when the tide is out.

Food from the Sea

The cooking of Brittany includes lots of fish and seafood. *Cotriade* is a fish stew made of conger eel and whatever else the fishermen caught and did not sell! It has potatoes in it, too. It is flavored with bouquet garni, which is a mix of tasty fresh herbs.

Roadside Pancakes

People in Brittany love to eat pancakes, called crepes, and pastries, called galettes. Little *creperies* can be found all over Brittany. They are small roadside cafés that serve pancakes.

Many people visit Brittany to see the amazing abbey of Mont-Saint-Michel.

Crepes are often served with fruit, syrup, and tasty ice cream.

Crepes

YOU WILL NEED:

1 cup all-purpose flour
1 tbsp superfine sugar
¼ tsp salt
1½ cups whole milk
4 eggs
3 tbsp unsalted butter, melted
fresh berries, to serve
mint sprigs and chocolate
    sauce, to decorate

Crepes make a wonderful dessert. The famous French recipe is crepes suzette. This is a light pancake that is cooked in an orange butter sauce, sprinkled with liqueur, and set on fire when it is served! You can serve your crepe with some yummy fresh fruit!

BE SAFE!
• Ask for help from a grown-up when using the blender.
• A grown-up should flip the crepes for you.

STEP 1

Place all the ingredients in a blender and blend until the mixture forms a smooth batter. Let the mixture stand for at least 15 minutes.

STEP 2

Heat a 12 inch (30 cm) pan and coat with butter. Ladle in enough batter to cover the base of the pan. Swirl to coat evenly. Cook until the underside is golden brown.

STEP 3

Loosen the edges of the crepe with a spatula, then flip it over. Cook on the second side for 1 minute more. Slide the crepe out of the pan and keep warm. Continue making crepes until the batter is used up. Add more butter to the pan as required.

STEP 4

Serve the crepes with fresh fruit, decorated with mint sprigs and chocolate sauce.

TOP TIP You can put the batter in the fridge for up to 24 hours in an airtight container. Remember to whisk it before cooking it.

French Meals on the Map!

Now that you have discovered how to cook the delicious foods of France, find out where they are cooked and eaten on this map of the country.

England

Brittany

Crepes

Bay of Biscay

ATLANTIC OCEAN

Truffade

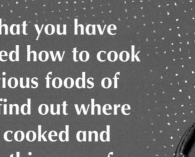

Quiche Lorraine

Lorraine

PARIS

Croque
Madame

Seine River

France

Auvergne

Italy

Ratatouille

Provence

Mediterranean
Sea

Glossary

abbey (A-bee) A house for people, such as monks or nuns, who have taken vows of faith.

croissants (kruh-SAWNTZ) Light, buttery pastries that are eaten for breakfast.

festival (FES-tih-vul) A large celebration in which many people take part.

gargoyles (GAR-goylz) Carved, animal-like figures with scary faces.

garnish (GAR-nish) To decorate food before serving.

gorges (GORJ-ez) Very deep gaps in Earth's surface, found between two cliff-like areas of ground.

ingredients (in-GREE-dee-untz) Different foods and seasonings that are used to make a recipe.

inlets (IN-lets) A gap in the coastline into which the ocean flows.

medieval (mee-DEE-vul) A time in history between the fifth and fifteenth centuries.

pâtés (pa-TAYZ) Smooth mixtures of meat, fish, beans, or vegetables that are usually eaten with bread or crackers.

quiche (KEESH) A dish made with a pastry base and a creamy filling.

rutabaga (roo-tuh-BAY-guh) A sweet-tasting root vegetable that is often used in stews.

sauté (saw-TAY) To lightly fry food in oil or butter.

sites (SYTS) Famous, often historical, places that people choose to visit.

vinaigrette (vih-nih-GREHT) A salad dressing made of vinegar, oil, and herbs.

volcanoes (vol-KAY-nohz) Openings in the Earth's crust from which lava flows.

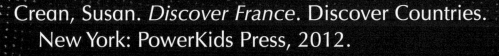
Further Reading

Crean, Susan. *Discover France*. Discover Countries. New York: PowerKids Press, 2012.

Wagner, Lisa. *Cool French Cooking: Fun and Tasty Recipes for Kids*. Cool World Cooking. Minneapolis, MN: Checkerboard Books, 2011.

Waldee, Lynne Marie. *Cooking the French Way*. Cooking Around the World. Minneapolis, MN: Lerner Publishing Group, 2009.

Websites

Due to the changing nature of Internet links, PowerKids Press has developed an online list of websites related to the subject of this book. This site is updated regularly. Please use this link to access the list:
www.powerkidslinks.com/caw/fren